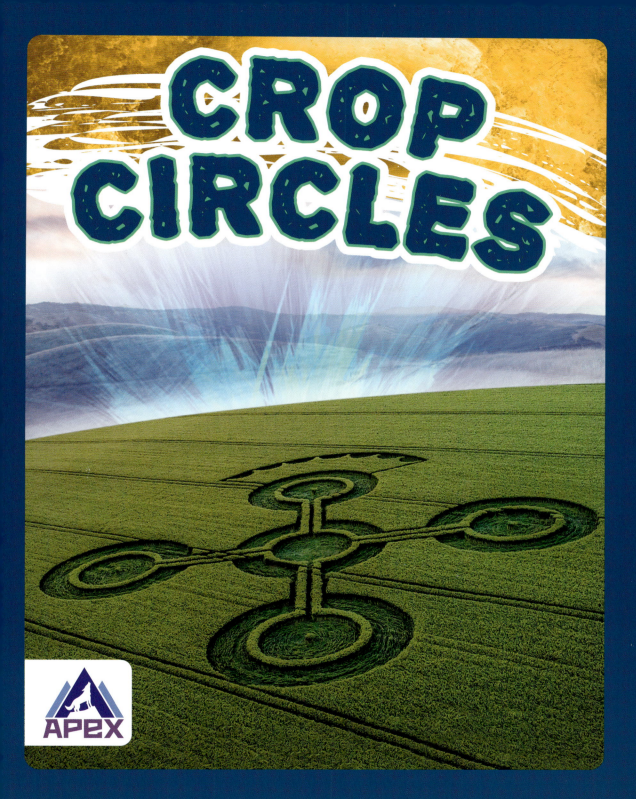

CROP CIRCLES

BY SUE GAGLIARDI

WWW.APEXEDITIONS.COM

Copyright © 2022 by Apex Editions, Mendota Heights, MN 55120. All rights reserved. No part of this book may be reproduced or utilized in any form or by any means without written permission from the publisher.

Apex is distributed by North Star Editions:
sales@northstareditions.com | 888-417-0195

Produced for Apex by Red Line Editorial.

Photographs ©: Shutterstock Images, cover (foreground), 1 (foreground), 4–5, 6–7, 8–9, 10–11, 14, 15, 18–19, 20, 21, 22–23, 24, 25, 26–27, 29; Unsplash, cover (background), 1 (background); iStockphoto, 12–13; Album/British Library/Alamy, 16–17

Library of Congress Control Number: 2021915679

ISBN
978-1-63738-161-8 (hardcover)
978-1-63738-197-7 (paperback)
978-1-63738-266-0 (ebook pdf)
978-1-63738-233-2 (hosted ebook)

Printed in the United States of America
Mankato, MN
012022

NOTE TO PARENTS AND EDUCATORS

Apex books are designed to build literacy skills in striving readers. Exciting, high-interest content attracts and holds readers' attention. The text is carefully leveled to allow students to achieve success quickly. Additional features, such as bolded glossary words for difficult terms, help build comprehension.

TABLE OF CONTENTS

CHAPTER 1
MYSTERY IN THE FIELDS 5

CHAPTER 2
WHAT ARE CROP CIRCLES? 11

CHAPTER 3
THE LEGEND'S HISTORY 17

CHAPTER 4
CROP CIRCLES EXPLAINED 23

Comprehension Questions • 28
Glossary • 30
To Learn More • 31
About the Author • 31
Index • 32

CHAPTER 1

MYSTERY IN THE FIELDS

A farmer wakes at dawn. He sets out to work in his fields. But a strange sight meets his eyes.

Crop circles often appear in fields of wheat, oats, or corn.

Several crop circles may join together to make larger shapes or patterns.

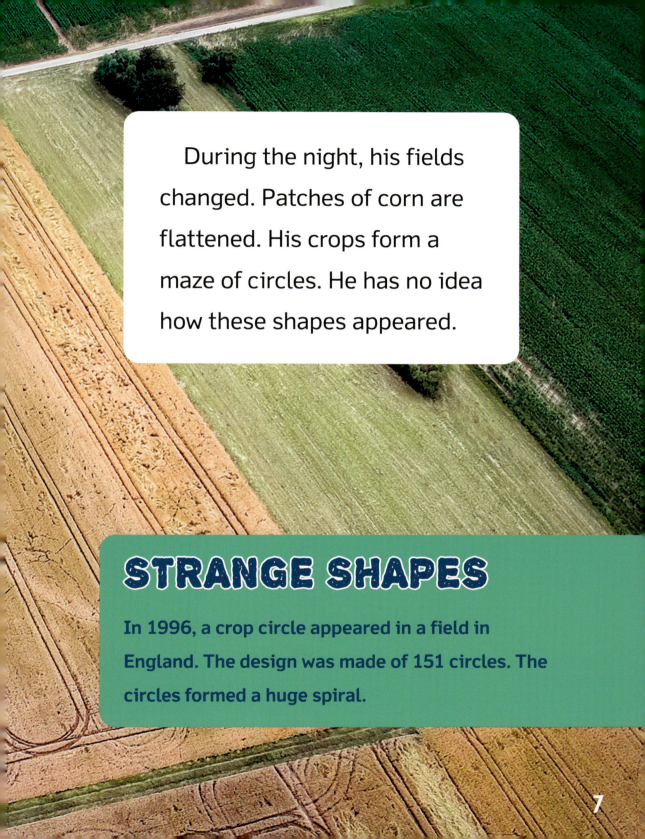

During the night, his fields changed. Patches of corn are flattened. His crops form a maze of circles. He has no idea how these shapes appeared.

STRANGE SHAPES

In 1996, a crop circle appeared in a field in England. The design was made of 151 circles. The circles formed a huge spiral.

His neighbor's fields have the same **eerie** shapes. She says they are crop circles. But she does not know where they came from either.

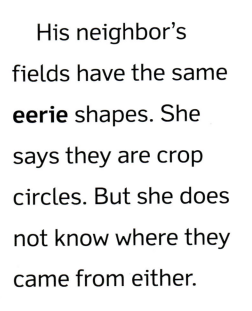

Some crop circles are just a few inches wide. Others are hundreds of feet across.

CHAPTER 2

WHAT ARE CROP CIRCLES?

Crop circles are **mysterious** patterns. They appear in fields at night. Some of the crops are flattened. The rest of the plants stay standing.

In most crop circles, the plants are not broken. They can continue to grow.

Many crop circles show up in England. But people have also found them in many other countries. Their shapes and sizes can vary, too.

SWIRLS AND SPIRALS

Most crop circles are single circles. But some circles overlap or form rings. In each circle, plants are bent down in a spiral pattern. The spirals can swirl in different directions.

Wiltshire County in England was the location of several famous crop circles.

Alien spaceships are often said to be smooth and round.

Some people say that **aliens** make crop circles. Their spaceships may flatten the plants when they land. Or the patterns may be secret messages.

Some patterns look like pictures or letters.

Crop circles may look like stars or flowers.

CHAPTER 3

THE LEGEND'S HISTORY

People have told stories of crop circles for hundreds of years. Early stories came from England. They told of a creature called the mowing devil. They said it cut patterns in farmers' fields.

An illustration from 1678 shows the mowing devil.

In the late 1900s, crop circles became very popular. People found them more often. They also appeared in more countries.

Most crop circles appear between April and September. This is the time of year when many crops grow.

18

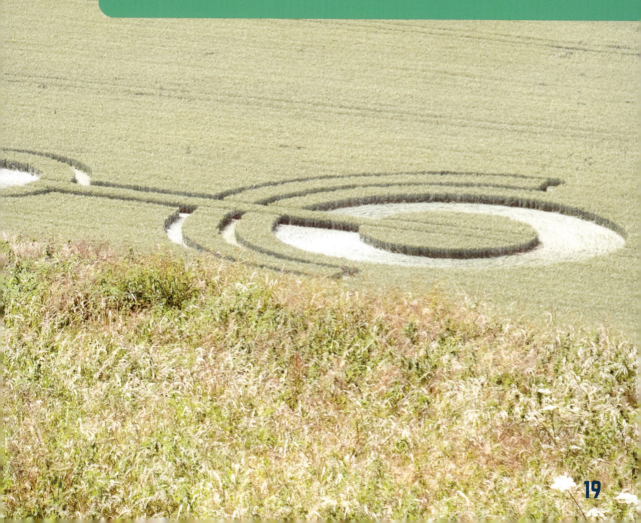

SPREADING STORIES

In 1980, an English farmer found three crop circles. Lots of people visited or wrote about them. They helped the **legend** spread around the world.

Newer circles often had **complex** designs. People said aliens made them. **Tourists** started coming to see them. Crop circles also appeared in books and movies.

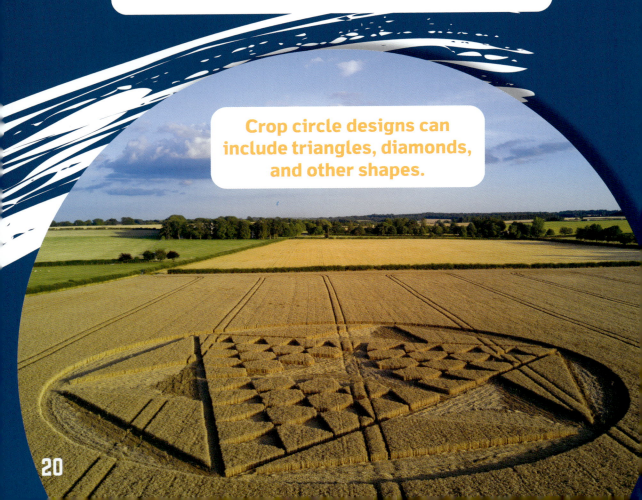

Crop circle designs can include triangles, diamonds, and other shapes.

People visit a huge crop circle in a cornfield in Germany.

By 1990, people were finding hundreds of crop circles each year.

CHAPTER 4
CROP CIRCLES EXPLAINED

People have many ideas about how and why crop circles appear. Some say the circles form when sick plants fall over. Others blame strong winds.

Fungus can harm a plant's roots, stems, or leaves. This kills or weakens the plant.

Animals might create the circles as they move or eat. However, these **theories** are hard to prove. People don't see the circles form.

Animals can trample plants as they graze in fields.

Hedgehogs are most active at night. They often make nests or burrows near farms or gardens.

Hedgehogs often run in circles. These animals might make crop circles.

In many cases, crop circles are **hoaxes**. **Evidence** shows that people made them. People may do this to trick or scare others.

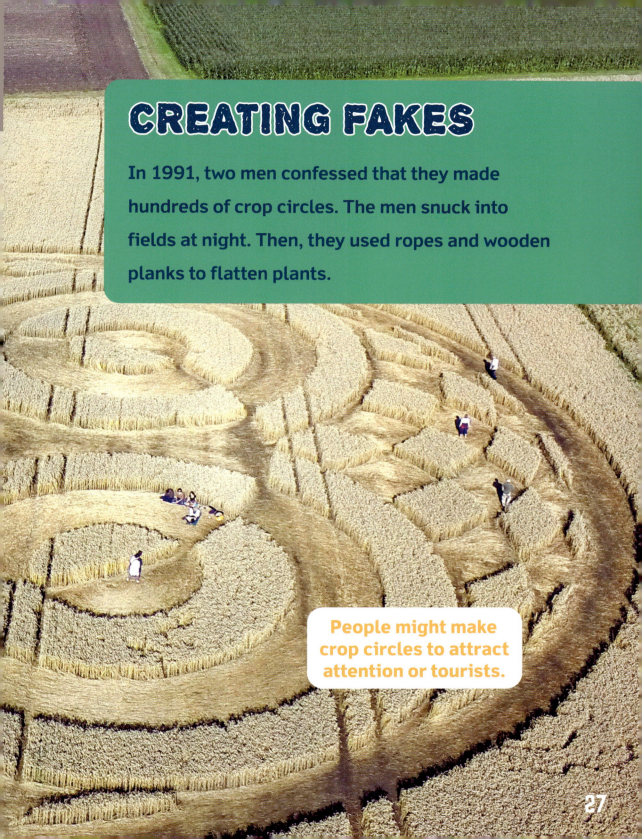

CREATING FAKES

In 1991, two men confessed that they made hundreds of crop circles. The men snuck into fields at night. Then, they used ropes and wooden planks to flatten plants.

People might make crop circles to attract attention or tourists.

COMPREHENSION QUESTIONS

Write your answers on a separate piece of paper.

1. Write a sentence describing what a crop circle is.

2. Would you want to see a crop circle up close? Why or why not?

3. According to early legends, what created crop circles?

   A. humans
   B. aliens
   C. the mowing devil

4. Why are theories about how crop circles form hard to prove?

   A. Crop circles only last a very short time.
   B. People can only read about crop circles online.
   C. People must guess what happens instead of watching it.

5. What does **design** mean in this book?

*The **design** was made of 151 circles. The circles formed a huge spiral.*

    A. a shape or pattern
    B. a very small piece
    C. a type of food

6. What does **popular** mean in this book?

*In the late 1900s, crop circles became very **popular**. People found them more often.*

    A. seen by no one
    B. known by many people
    C. known by fewer people

Answer key on page 32.

29

GLOSSARY

aliens
Creatures that come from planets other than Earth.

complex
Having many parts or pieces.

eerie
Strange or scary.

evidence
Information that tells what happened or if something
is true.

hoaxes
Tricks to make people believe something that is not true.

legend
A famous story, often based on facts but not always
completely true.

mysterious
Hard to explain or understand.

theories
Guesses about how or why something happens.

tourists
People who visit a place for fun.

TO LEARN MORE

BOOKS

O'Keefe, Emily. *Investigating Crop Circles*. New York: AV2 by Weigl, 2020.

Reed, Ellis M. *Alien Conspiracy Theories*. North Mankato, MN: Capstone Press, 2020.

Steinkraus, Kyla. *Crop Circles*. Mankato, MN: Black Rabbit Books, 2018.

ONLINE RESOURCES

Visit **www.apexeditions.com** to find links and resources related to this title.

ABOUT THE AUTHOR

Sue Gagliardi writes fiction, nonfiction, and poetry for children. She enjoys learning about mysterious legends and exploring new places.

INDEX

A
aliens, 14, 20
animals, 24–25

E
England, 7, 12, 17

F
farmers, 5, 17, 19
fields, 5, 7–8, 11,
   17, 27

H
hoaxes, 26

M
messages, 14
mowing devil, 17

P
patterns, 11–12,
   14–15, 17
pictures, 15

R
rings, 12

S
shapes, 7–8, 12
sick plants, 23
spaceships, 14
spirals, 7, 12

T
theories, 24
tourists, 20

W
winds, 23

Answer Key:
1. Answers will vary; **2.** Answers will vary; **3.** C; **4.** C; **5.** A; **6.** B